ALL the BIRDS in the WORLD

David Opie

What about me?

PETER PAUPER PRESS, INC.
WHITE PLAINS, NEW YORK

Published by Peter Pauper Press, Inc.
202 Mamaroneck Avenue
White Plains, New York 10601 USA

Library of Congress Control Number: 2019951470

ISBN 978-1-4413-3329-2
Manufactured for Peter Pauper Press, Inc.
Printed in Hong Kong

7 6 5 4 3 2 1

Visit us at www.peterpauper.com

To my wonderful wife, Miller

All birds have feathers.
All birds have wings.
All birds have beaks.

But birds come in many colors.
There are gray birds, brown ones,
black, gold, and white.
Some birds have red wings,
or a blazing orange body,
or a ruby throat.
They seem to be painted
with more colors
than you can see.

"But what about me?"
asked Kiwi.

Birds vary in shape and size.
Some have crests, crowns, scissor-tails,
or short, stumpy bodies.
An ostrich can stand taller
than the tallest basketball player,
while some hummingbirds
are about as long as your pinkie finger.

Some birds, like storks, flamingos, egrets, and cranes,
have long legs like stilts,
so they can wade in water
and hunt for food.

"But what about me?" asked Kiwi.

Most birds make their own homes.
Eagles build huge nests,
and some hummingbirds weave
their tiny nests together
using silk from spider webs.
Sociable Weavers make nests
that take up whole trees
and house an entire community.

"But what about me?" asked Kiwi.

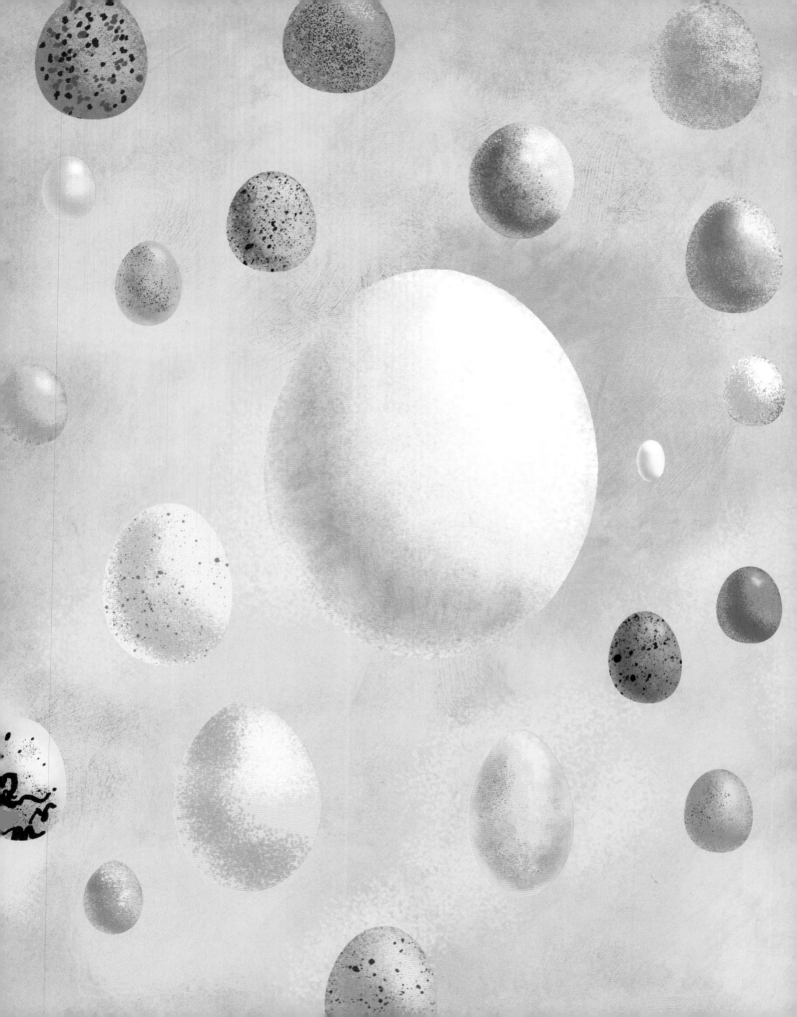

All birds come from eggs.
Birds' eggs come in assorted sizes and colors
just like birds.
Eggs can be speckled brown
or sky blue
and many colors in between.
Hummingbird eggs
are about the size of a jelly bean,
while ostrich eggs
are as big as a cantaloupe.

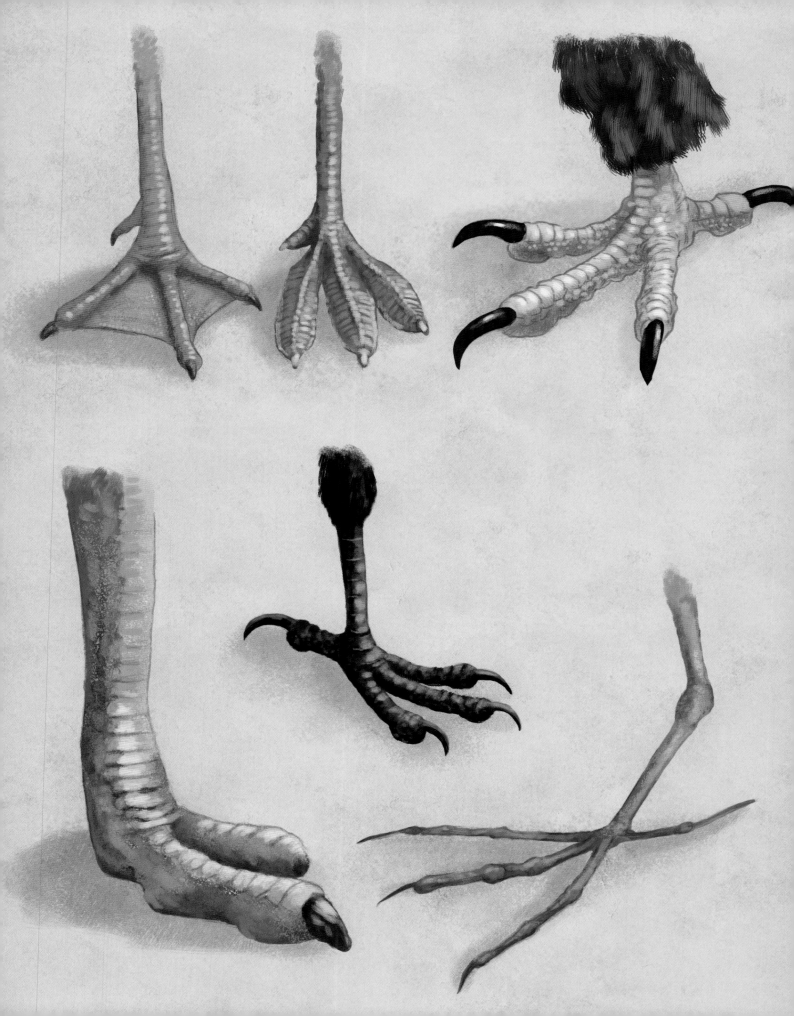

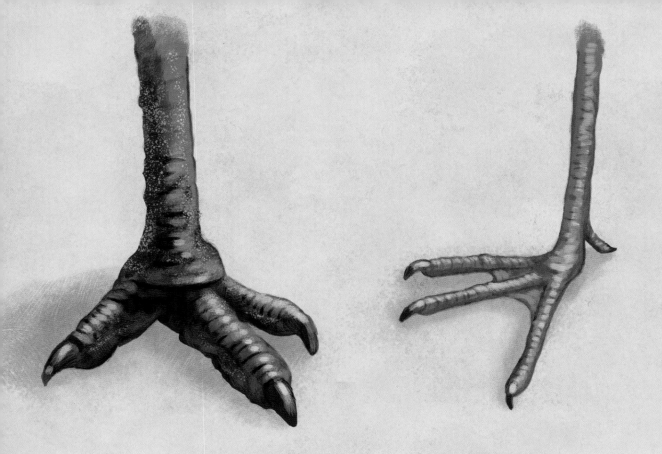

Birds' feet are more like claws.
They use them to scratch, perch, swim, grab,
tear, hop, dig, run, hold, grasp, and fight.

Most birds have four toes,
but the ostrich has only two,
and many others have three.

"How many
do I see?"
asked Kiwi.

All birds have beaks
of different shapes and sizes.
Birds use their beaks to smash seeds,
tear apart meat, sip plant nectar,
gulp down fish, and hammer into wood
to get grubs.

And what's the most amazing thing
birds can do?
They fly, fly, fly!
Because birds have wings.
Don't you wish
you could fly?

Some birds migrate,
which means they fly great distances
for food and nesting
when the seasons change.

"But what
about me?"
asked Kiwi.

Many birds float and swim,
or dive underwater for fish,
shooting through the water
like feathered torpedoes.

"I think I can swim," said Kiwi.

Some birds are nocturnal,
which means they are active
when most other birds are sleeping.
They have big eyes
for seeing in the dark.
They hunt and migrate
under the cover of night.

"Even me?" asked Kiwi.

Birds call and sing
beautiful songs.
They sing for a mate
and warn rivals away.
They warble, tweet, chirp, trill,
cheep, peep, and scream.
Yes, hawks scream.
And seagulls laugh.
Emus drum and boom
and can be heard a mile away.

"But what
about me?"
asked Kiwi.

Ah, yes,
and there's even a bird,
found only in New Zealand—
the kiwi!
It lays very large eggs
compared to its body size,
and lives in an underground burrow,
instead of nesting in trees.
The kiwi has no tail,
but has whiskers like a cat,
and has soft, fur-like feathers,
nostrils at the tip of a long, skinny beak,
tiny, hidden wings,
and does not fly.

All birds have feathers.
All birds have wings.
All birds have beaks.

And all the birds
in this book,
all the gulls, finches, owls, eagles, hawks, egrets,
ducks, sparrows, pigeons, turkeys, hummingbirds, jays,
herons, chickadees, swifts, parrots, ostriches, storks, geese,
and all the other types of birds in the world,
are part of the same feathered family!

"Even me!" said Kiwi.

Yes, even Kiwi.

A Note from the Author

Birds have always fascinated me. When I was a kid, I would grab my binoculars and my *Peterson Field Guide to Birds* and go "birding" in the woods behind my house. Whenever I found a feather, I placed it between the pages of the type of bird that it came from. I kept a "life list" of all the ones I'd seen. Of course, I haven't come close to seeing the estimated 10,000 types of birds believed to be living in the world today. My favorite bird fact is that they are evolved from dinosaurs. That's right—birds are their direct descendants! Take a look at the dinosaur "Archaeopteryx" to see an ancient bird relative. And the next time you spot a bird, think to yourself, "There goes a modern-day dinosaur!"

Cover

1. Great Cormorant
2. Barn Owl
3. American Goldfinch
4. Ring-necked Pheasant
5. Sandhill Crane
6. Turkey Vulture
7. European Starling
8. Scissor-tailed Flycatcher
9. Rosy-faced Lovebird
10. Canada Goose
11. Black-capped Chickadee
12. Northern Mockingbird
13. American Woodcock
14. Pileated Woodpecker
15. Herring Gull
16. Great Horned Owl
17. Canada Goose
18. Snowy Egret
19. Ruby-throated Hummingbird
20. Red-Winged Blackbird
21. Herring Gull
22. American Flamingo
23. Eastern Bluebird
24. Canary

25. Painted Bunting
26. Amur Falcon
27. Monk Parakeet
28. Arctic Tern
29. American Robin
30. Northern Cardinal
31. Mallard Duck
32. Blue Jay
33. Wood Duck
34. Keel-billed Toucan
35. Laughing Gull
36. Osprey
37. Scarlet Macaw
38. Belted Kingfisher
39. Baltimore Oriole
40. Cedar Waxwing
41. Red-masked Parakeet
42. Atlantic Puffin
43. Great Indian Hornbill
44. Rock Pigeon
45. Eastern Bluebird
46. Mourning Dove
47. Brown Kiwi

Pages 2-3   Indian Peacock and Brown Kiwi

Some birds in the background are not identified. Not necessarily to scale.

Pages 4-5

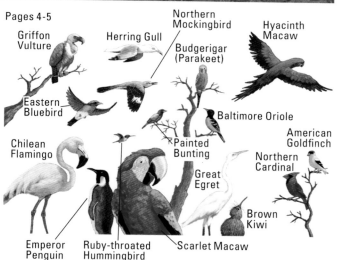

Griffon Vulture

Herring Gull

Northern Mockingbird

Hyacinth Macaw

Budgerigar (Parakeet)

Eastern Bluebird

Baltimore Oriole

Chilean Flamingo

Painted Bunting

American Goldfinch

Northern Cardinal

Great Egret

Emperor Penguin

Ruby-throated Hummingbird

Scarlet Macaw

Brown Kiwi

Pages 6-7   Left to right: Common Ostrich, Brown Kiwi, Bee Hummingbird (flying), Scissor-tailed Flycatcher (flying), Great Gray Owl, Belted Kingfisher, Great Blue Heron, Tawny Frogmouth (on branch)

Pages 8-9   Left to right: Snowy Egret, Black-necked Stilt, Roseate Spoonbill, Sandhill Crane, Glossy Ibis, Wood Stork, Brown Kiwi, American Flamingo

Pages 10-11

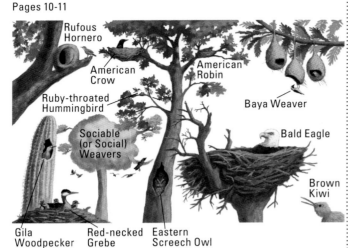

Rufous Hornero
American Crow
Ruby-throated Hummingbird
American Robin
Baya Weaver
Sociable (or Social) Weavers
Bald Eagle
Brown Kiwi
Gila Woodpecker
Red-necked Grebe
Eastern Screech Owl

Pages 12-13

Ostrich egg
Hummingbird egg
Brown Kiwi

Pages 14-15   Top row, left to right: Duck, Grebe, Eagle, Emu, Willet
Bottom row, left to right: Ostrich, Crow, Jacana, Brown Kiwi

Pages 16-17

Brown Pelican
Grey Fantail
Blue-and-gold Macaw
Shoebill
American Crow
Northern Cardinal
White Ibis
Toco Toucan
Roseate Spoonbill
Great Blue Heron
Ruby-throated Hummingbird
Bald Eagle
Brown Kiwi
Great Horned Owl
Pileated Woodpecker

Pages 18-19

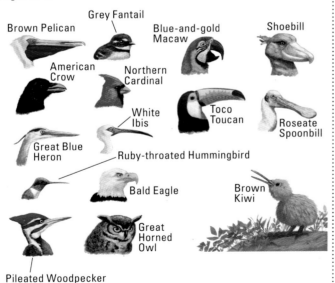

1
2
3
4
5
6
7
8
9
10
11
12
13
14
15
16
17
18
19
20
21
22

1. Red-headed Woodpecker
2. American Kestrel
3. Yellow Warbler
4. Scarlet Tanager
5. Osprey
6. Black-browed Albatross
7. Turkey Vulture
8. Arctic Tern
9. Barn Swallow
10. American Woodcock
11. Canada Goose
12. Brown Pelican
13. Baltimore Oriole
14. Eastern Bluebird
15. Barn Owl
16. Common Kingfisher
17. Laughing Gull
18. Mallard Duck
19. Broad-billed Hummingbird
20. Northern Mockingbird
21. Northern Cardinal
22. Brown Kiwi

Pages 20-21   Left to right, top: Brown Pelican, Common Loon, Mute Swan, Brown Kiwi
Left to right, underwater: Double-crested Cormorant, Anhinga, African Penguin (above), King Penguins (below)

Pages 22-23   Left to right: Great Horned Owl (on tree limb), Black-crowned Night Heron, Whip-poor-will, Common Potoo, Barn Owl (in flight), Brown Kiwi

Pages 24-25

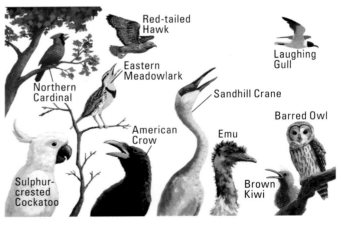

Red-tailed Hawk
Laughing Gull
Eastern Meadowlark
Sandhill Crane
Northern Cardinal
Barred Owl
American Crow
Emu
Sulphur-crested Cockatoo
Brown Kiwi

Snow Goose

Turkey Vulture

Red-crowned Amazon Parrot

Willet

Mallard Duck

Blue Jay

Herring Gull

Scarlet Macaw

Northern Flicker

Short-tailed Albatross

Arctic Tern

Great Cormorant

Snowy Owl

European Starling

Canada Goose

Herring Gull

American Crow

Rock Pigeon

Ruby-throated Hummingbird

Wild Turkey

Ruffed Grouse

Ring-necked Pheasant

Killdeer

Brown Kiwi

Common Ostrich

King Penguin

Great Blue Heron

Emperor Penguin chick

Snowy Egret

Wood Stork

1. Song Sparrow
2. Northern Cardinal
3. Baltimore Oriole
4. Bald Eagle
5. Belted Kingfisher
6. Eastern Phoebe
7. Northern Saw-whet Owl
8. Purple Finch
9. Scarlet Tanager
10. Downy Woodpecker
11. Great Horned Owl
12. Evening Grosbeak
13. Common Grackle

14. Mourning Dove
15. American Goldfinch
16. Indigo Bunting
17. Peregrine Falcon
18. Gray Catbird
19. Red-winged Blackbird
20. Northern Mockingbird
21. Red-tailed Hawk
22. Black-capped Chickadee
23. Wood Thrush
24. American Robin
25. Eastern Bluebird

Some birds in the background are not identified. Not necessarily to scale.

More about Kiwis

Kiwis are very interesting birds found only on the islands that make up New Zealand. They are about the size of a chicken. Kiwis belong to a group of birds called "ratites," which includes other flightless birds like the ostrich, emu, rhea, and cassowary. Before certain non-native animals (like dogs and weasels) were introduced to New Zealand, kiwis had few predators, and so they thrived without being able to fly. They do, however, have tiny, hidden wing buds. Their soft coat of feathers seems a lot like fur. They are the only bird that has nostrils at the tip of their long beak, which they use to sniff for insects. They have a piercing call. Kiwis have no tail, but they do have whiskers to help them feel their way through the dark of night, when they are most active. Although they generally don't spend a lot of time in water, kiwis can swim. Kiwis have powerful legs and four toes on each foot. They are fast runners. They build burrows in the ground. They also lay eggs that are very large in comparison to their body size. There are several different species of kiwi: Little Spotted, Great Spotted, Tokoeka, Rowi, and Brown. The kiwi that is the star of this book is a Brown Kiwi.

Kiwi species (from left to right): Great Spotted, Little Spotted, Tokoeka, Brown, Rowi